Why Do I Yawn?

by Molly Kolpin

Consulting Editor: Gail Saunders-Smith, PhD

Consultant: Marjorie Hogan, MD
Department of Pediatrics
Hennepin County Medical Center

Pebble®
Plus

CAPSTONE PRESS
a capstone imprint

Pebble Plus is published by Capstone Press,
1710 Roe Crest Drive, North Mankato, Minnesota 56003
www.capstonepub.com

Library of Congress Cataloging-in-Publication Data
Kolpin, Molly, author.
Why do I yawn? / by Molly Kolpin.
pages cm. — (Pebble plus. My silly body)
Summary: "Simple text and full-page photos describe the theories about why people yawn"— Provided by publisher.
Audience: Ages 4–8.
Audience: K to grade 3.
Includes bibliographical references and index.
ISBN 978-1-4914-2107-9 (library binding)
ISBN 978-1-4914-2348-6 (eBook PDF)
1. Yawning—Juvenile literature. 2. Respiration—Juvenile literature. 3. Human physiology—Juvenile literature. I. Title.
QP372.K57 2015
612.2'1—dc23   2014022197

Editorial Credits
Michelle Hasselius, editor; Kazuko Collins, designer; Gina Kammer, media researcher; Morgan Walters, production specialist

Photo Credits
iStockphotos: EyeJoy, 15; Shutterstock: CLIPAREA l Custom media, 11, Digital Media Pro, 9, DoctorKan, 17, Gelpi JM, cover, Gelpi JM, 21, MAHATHIR MOHD YASIN, 19, Marko Tomicic, 13, Oksana Kuzmina, 5, Radharani, 7
Design Elements: Shutterstock: froe_mic (spotted background), xtremelife (red sunburst)

Note to Parents and Teachers

The My Silly Body set supports national science standards related to life science. This book describes and illustrates why we yawn. The images support early readers in understanding the text. The repetition of words and phrases helps early readers learn new words. This book also introduces early readers to subject-specific vocabulary words, which are defined in the Glossary section. Early readers may need assistance to read some words and to use the Table of Contents, Glossary, Read More, Internet Sites, and Index sections of the book.

Printed in the United States of America in Stevens Point, Wisconsin
102014   008479WZS15

Table of Contents

Wake Up!

Why do I yawn?

Nobody knows for sure why

humans and animals yawn.

But scientists have some ideas.

Animals such as cats and dogs yawn.

When you yawn, you open your mouth and take in a deep breath of air. The air fills your lungs and stretches the muscles in your stomach.

A yawn lasts about six seconds.

Yawning speeds up your heart rate and makes you feel more alert. Some scientists think you yawn to wake up when you're tired.

If you don't sleep well at night, you may yawn more during the day.

9

Keeping Cool

Another idea is that yawning cools your brain. Your brain has more energy in cooler temperatures. So yawning might help you think more clearly.

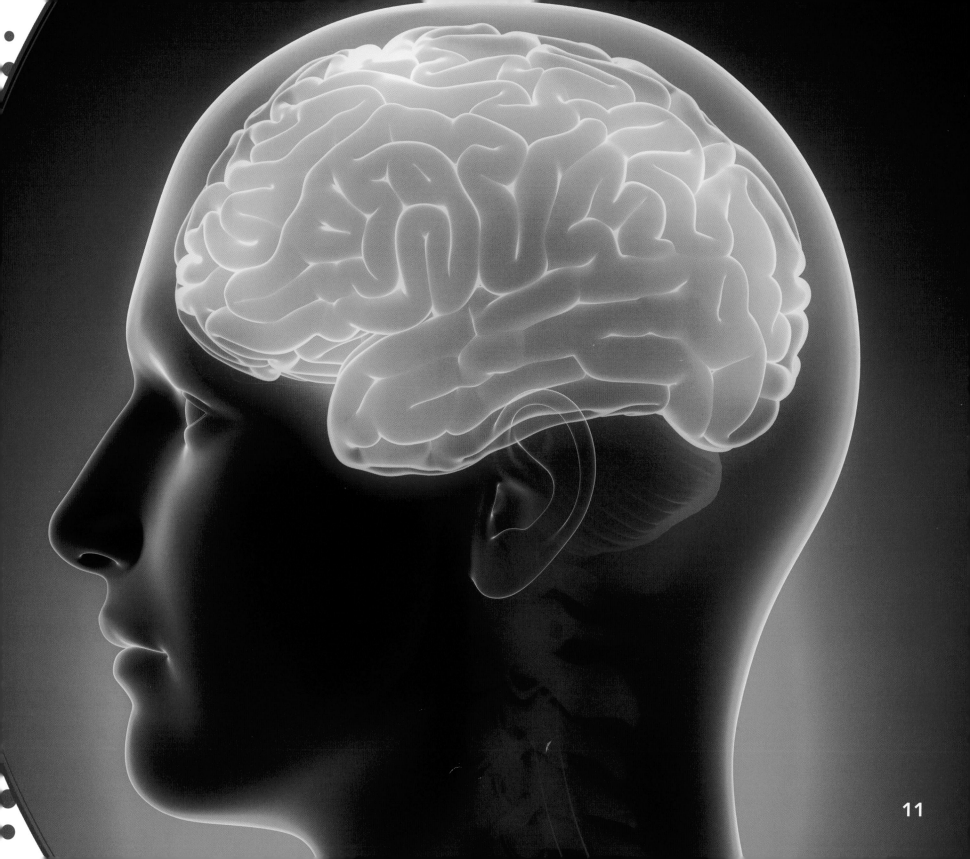

How does this theory work? When you yawn you take in a breath of air. The cold air cools your brain. Studies show people yawn more in cold weather.

Pay attention to when you yawn the most. Are you cold or warm?

Bonding by Yawning

It may not be clear why you yawn, but one thing is for sure—yawns are contagious! This means if you see a friend yawn, you'll probably yawn too.

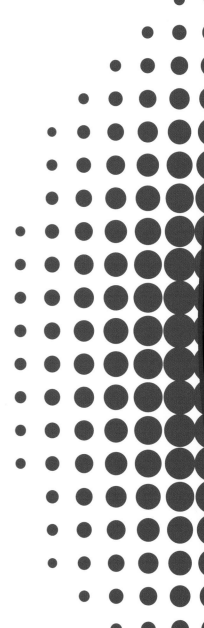

Yawns may be used to communicate. You yawn when you're bored or tired. People yawn back to show they feel the same way.

Thinking or reading about yawning can cause you to yawn.

Before there were clocks,
seeing others yawn let
everyone know it was
time to go to sleep.

Mystery Unsolved

Maybe one day you'll solve the yawning mystery. For now be polite and cover your mouth when you yawn!

When you feel a yawn coming on, cover your mouth and yawn quietly.

Glossary

alert—awake and paying attention

communicate—to share thoughts, feelings, or information with other people

contagious—able to be spread between people

energy—the strength to do activities without feeling tired

heart rate—the number of times a person's heart beats per minute

muscle—a part of the body that helps you move, lift, or push

mystery—something that is hard to explain or understand

polite—having good manners

scientist—a person who studies facts and the world around us

studies—a detailed testing of a subject or situation

theory—an idea that explains something that is unknown

Read More

Schwinn, Aleaha. *What Happens When I Yawn?* My Body Does Strange Stuff! New York: Gareth Stevens Publishing, 2014.

Nicolson, Cynthia Pratt. *Totally Human: Why We Look and Act the Way We Do.* Tonawanda, N.Y.: Kids Can Press Ltd., 2011.

Reina, Mary. *A Tour of Your Respiratory System.* Body Systems. North Mankato, Minn.: Capstone Press, 2013.

Internet Sites

FactHound offers a safe, fun way to find Internet sites related to this book. All of the sites on FactHound have been researched by our staff.

Here's all you do:
Visit *www.facthound.com*
Type in this code: 9781491421079

Super-cool stuff! Check out projects, games and lots more at www.capstonekids.com

Critical Thinking Using the Common Core

Scientists have many theories about why we yawn. What is a theory? (Craft and Structure)

Yawning can be used to communicate. What is one message we can send to others by yawning? Use the text to help you with your answer. (Key Ideas and Details)

Index

Word Count: 209
Grade: 1
Early-Intervention Level: 21